Date: 9/6/22

**PALM BEACH COUNTY
LIBRARY SYSTEM**

**3650 Summit Boulevard
West Palm Beach, FL 33406**

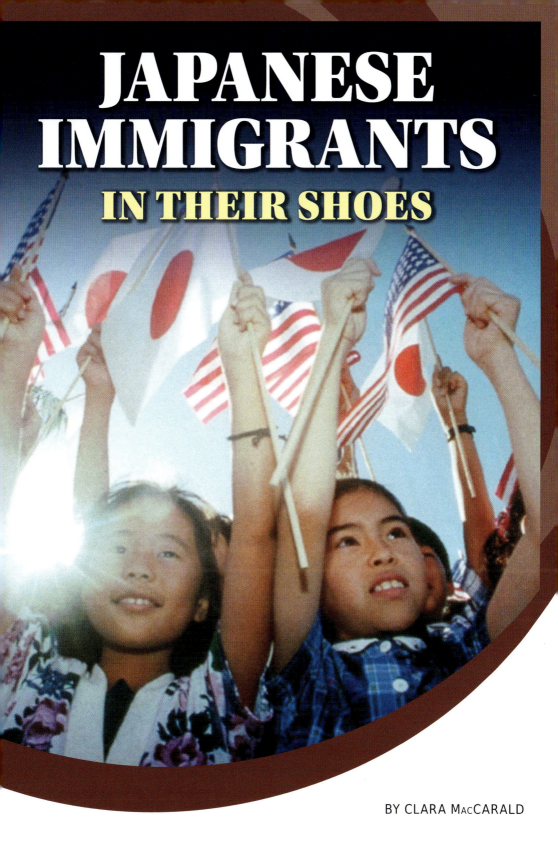

JAPANESE IMMIGRANTS
IN THEIR SHOES

BY CLARA MacCARALD

Published by The Child's World®
1980 Lookout Drive • Mankato, MN 56003-1705
800-599-READ • www.childsworld.com

Content Consultant: Sidney X. Lu, PhD, Assistant Professor of History, Michigan State University

Photographs ©: Bob Galbraith/AP Images, cover, 1; iStockphoto, 6; Hawaii State Archives/AP Images, 9; AP Images, 10, 23; Red Line Editorial, 13; Bettmann/Getty Images, 14, 17, 19; Everett Historical/Shutterstock Images, 20; Kyodo/AP Images, 25; John Hayes/AP Images, 26; Lenny Ignelzi/AP Images, 28

ISBN 9781503820272
LCCN 2016960929

Printed in the United States of America
PA02338

ABOUT THE AUTHOR

Clara MacCarald is a freelance writer with a master's degree in biology who writes educational books for children. She has also written about news and science for local publications in central New York. She belongs to the National Association of Science Writers and the Society of Children's Book Writers and Illustrators.

TABLE OF CONTENTS

FAST FACTS

Important Years

- Immigration of Japanese men peaked between 1885 and 1908 as Japanese men sought out jobs that could earn more money.

- Immigration of Japanese women peaked between 1908 and 1920 as Japanese picture brides traveled to be with their newly arranged Japanese husbands.

Important Numbers

- Between 1885 and 1924, approximately 200,000 Japanese people immigrated to Hawaii.

- During this time, another 180,000 Japanese people went to the U.S. mainland.

Reasons for Japanese Immigration

- Most Japanese immigrants were looking for opportunities to make money.

- Some Japanese immigrants, such as picture brides, were joining new spouses.

TIMELINE

1885: The first large group of Japanese immigrants sets sail for Hawaii.

1900: The U.S. government ends **contract labor** in Hawaii.

1908: Japan agrees to limit immigration to the United States. Japanese students are allowed in public schools of San Francisco, California.

1922: The U.S. Supreme Court rules that Japanese immigrants cannot become U.S. citizens because they are not white.

1924: The U.S. Congress stops Japanese immigration to the United States.

1941: The United States enters World War II (1939–1945).

1942: U.S. President Franklin D. Roosevelt sends Japanese Americans to **internment camps**.

1945: Japan surrenders, ending World War II.

1952: The U.S. Congress passes a law allowing Japanese immigrants to become U.S. citizens.

1988: The U.S. government apologizes for sending Japanese Americans to camps.

Chapter 1

ISLAND WORK

In 1896, a steamship called the *China-go* sailed into Honolulu, Hawaii. Steep volcanic peaks rose behind the port. Yasutaro Soga gathered his baggage. Like most early **issei**, or first-generation Japanese immigrants, Soga was a young man. He planned to work and study overseas before returning to his home in Japan.

For more than a decade, large numbers of Japanese had been coming to Hawaii. At the time, Hawaii was an independent kingdom. However, it was heavily influenced by Americans who owned most of the sugar **plantations** in the country. Japanese laborers could earn higher wages in Hawaii than they could in Japan. Hawaii welcomed Asian immigrants. The sugar industry considered Asian immigrants cheap labor.

Walking with the other passengers, Soga carried his belongings along the pier. The passengers headed to the immigration **quarantine** quarter, where they would stay until officials determined they were free of diseases. Inside, rows of boards were made into bunk beds. Soga thought it looked like a jail.

After several days, the quarantine quarter let Soga go. But the immigration process was not over yet. First, he had to show he had saved enough money to support himself while waiting for a job. He carefully handed over his large bundle of bills to an official. The official yelled that he had no time to count them. He threw the money back at Soga. "His rudeness made me very upset," Soga said. "But I kept silent to avoid further trouble."[1]

Soga had paid for the passage and brought money with him. That meant he could work for whomever he wished. He soon became the manager of a plantation store.

Other issei were not so lucky. In exchange for passage to Hawaii, many issei became contract laborers. That meant they had to work for a number of years to pay off the trip. Runaway contract laborers could be returned to their plantation or even jailed.

Mornings on the sugar plantation began early. The sound of a whistle woke the workers at 5:00 in the morning. The workers headed to the fields in the dark. Overseers watched them from horseback. One man complained, "If we talked too much, the man swung the whip. He did not actually whip us but just swung his whip so that we would work harder."[2]

Sugarcane stalks towered over the workers. The sharp leaves cut their hands as they worked in the hot, humid air. Those hoeing weeds had to bend over for hours. At 4:30 p.m., a whistle signaled the end of work.

Hawaii became part of the United States in 1900, and contract labor was illegal under U.S. law. Japanese immigrants continued going to Hawaii, but many moved to the West Coast of the United States looking for higher wages.

▲ **Immigrant workers spent long days in Hawaii's sugarcane fields.**

Soga found his place in Hawaii. He became a journalist and a writer in the Japanese community. He started a family and finally became a U.S. citizen in the early 1950s when he was in his late seventies. Like Soga, many of the issei lived the rest of their lives in their new country.

Chapter 2

SETTLING THE WEST COAST

In the spring of 1905, 17-year-old Nisuke Mitsumori arrived in San Francisco, California. The city's many piers were buzzing with activity. Mitsumori boarded a one-horse carriage, planning to ride to a Japanese inn. Suddenly, a gang of white teenagers appeared and started yelling insults at Mitsumori. The driver spurred on his horse while the teenagers threw **manure** at the carriage.

"This was my very first impression of America," said Mitsumori.[3] Originally, he had wanted to attend high school in Japan. But he moved to the United States to avoid being forced to serve in the Japanese military.

Safe at the inn, Mitsumori met some Japanese youths who worked at a newspaper. They invited him to the newspaper office where he found a job. Sometimes Japanese people came to the office with bruises from being beaten up. At the time, many white people feared the issei, both as competitors for jobs and as citizens of a powerful country, Japan. Mitsumori learned to walk carefully around town.

Mitsumori soon realized that his experience was not unique. Many new arrivals found work through other issei. Most large cities on the West Coast had Japanese inns, restaurants, and shops. Although some issei worked at these businesses, most ended up on the move, providing **migratory** labor.

Sadame Inouye was one of these laborers. He moved to the United States as a teenager, hoping to earn money to pay off his family's debts. After a night at a San Francisco inn, Inouye and a friend took a boat inland. The spring air chilled them as they traveled to the labor camp where they planned to work.

They sailed through two large bays and entered a maze of river channels.

Night fell, and Inouye and his friend made their way to an island where they found a warehouse to sleep in. They woke to chickens clucking. Other laborers who had slept in the warehouse helped them find their labor camp. They first worked in onion fields. After a month, Inouye moved on to potatoes and then to grapes. "When I worked here and there, I carried my own blanket roll with me and slept where I could," he said.[4]

Summer in California's valleys meant fiercely hot days. And conditions were just as difficult for issei working in other jobs. During the winter, issei railroad workers in the mountains braved temperatures below freezing. The hard work paid off for some. They often used their wages to buy or lease farmland. In fact, one of the farms that Inouye worked on was owned by a Japanese man.

But similar to all issei, Inouye started noticing an increase in anti-Japanese feelings and actions among many Americans. White people excluded Japanese immigrants from many jobs. In some places, mobs attacked or threatened the issei. In 1906, the city of San Francisco decided to send Asian children to separate schools from white children. Japan's government complained, leading to talks with the U.S. government.

In 1908, Japan agreed to limit new immigration. In return, the United States agreed that the issei would be treated better.

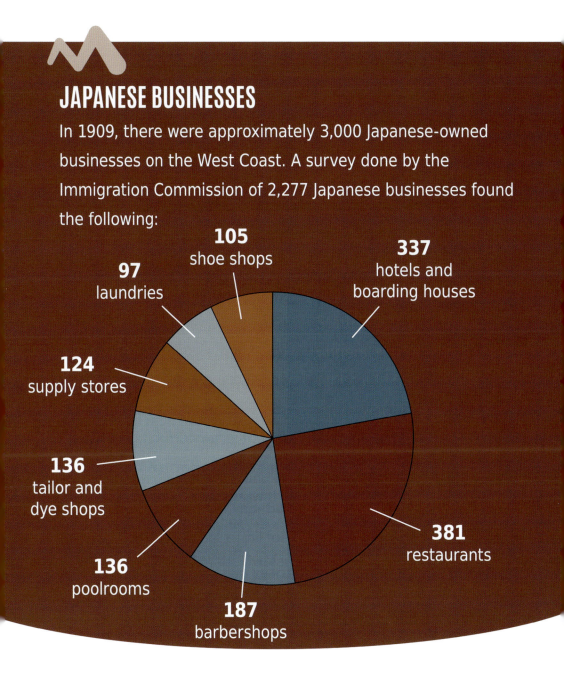

JAPANESE BUSINESSES

In 1909, there were approximately 3,000 Japanese-owned businesses on the West Coast. A survey done by the Immigration Commission of 2,277 Japanese businesses found the following:

105 shoe shops

97 laundries

337 hotels and boarding houses

124 supply stores

136 tailor and dye shops

381 restaurants

136 poolrooms

187 barbershops

Chapter 3

PICTURE BRIDES

In 1916, Asayo Noji prepared to board a steamship in Kobe, Japan. The 19-year-old cried as her parents and relatives saw her off. They told her to take good care of herself and to hurry home. Although Noji was sad to leave her family, she also felt optimism about where she was headed. "I had heard that America was a land of richness and a large country, so I was happy to be coming," she later wrote.[5]

While the ship traveled across the ocean, Noji had time to reflect on how she had gotten here. She was a picture bride. Relatives had arranged her marriage to an issei man in Oregon by exchanging pictures with him. Noji's wedding had already taken place in Japan with her husband's family. Now she was traveling to the United States to meet her husband.

Noji knew that the issei had communities, jobs, land, and businesses in the United States. Many issei men had decided to raise families in the United States rather than returning to Japan. They asked their relatives to help them find women. Although Japan limited immigration to the United States after 1908, the Japanese government allowed spouses and close relatives of the issei to go. So, between 1908 and 1920, young picture brides filled steamships headed to the United States.

Noji thought her ship was pretty, but it also stank. The odor of a new coat of tan paint mixed with the smells of oil and machinery. Powerful ocean waves rocked the boat, making some passengers seasick.

One day, the picture brides gathered around a group of issei men on the ship. Japanese who had already immigrated to the United States, like these men, were allowed to leave and return.

The issei men told the women to look carefully at the pictures of their husbands. Make sure to meet the right man, they warned. Some men looking for wives were not completely truthful. For example, a man might send an old photo, making himself seem much younger than he really was. Others had their photos changed to hide flaws or hair loss. Some made themselves sound richer or more important than they were.

Noji arrived at the immigration center in Seattle, Washington. On the second day, her husband arrived. Noji was dressed in a Japanese robe called a kimono. He wore an American suit with stripes. Noji was satisfied with him, although he looked thinner than his picture. Some brides fainted or even returned to Japan after meeting their husbands.

Noji was not impressed with the United States. She had expected a land full of wealth, but her new surroundings were poor. After a wagon ride over a dirt road through thick woods, she and her husband arrived home. "I had such a lonesome feeling," she said, "because I had never seen such a small house!"[6] All the furniture was unfamiliar. Her husband had to teach her to cook and bake in the American-style kitchen.

Other picture brides had similar stories. When Tei Endow arrived in Odell, Oregon, in 1918, her luggage was full of fashionable clothes. She soon found she didn't need them.

▲ Japanese brides line up for inspection after arriving in the United States.

She and her husband didn't get many visitors at their lonely house in the hills. In Japan, Endow had had electricity and running water. In the United States she had only oil lamps, a well, and an outhouse. Her family had owned a grocery store back home. Here she had to work hard weeding strawberry patches.

> "Life in the countryside was very lonesome. We moved from one farm to another. We worked at the Fair Ranch for a month, picked grapes in Florin, and then went to another work camp. . . . Sometimes we slept in a barn with horses and cows. We led that kind of life until our children were born."
>
> —*Takae Washizu, who landed in San Francisco in 1921 to be with her husband*[8]

Another picture bride, Ai Miyasaki, almost left because she felt so lonely. Her husband owned a restaurant near Reno, Nevada. Miyasaki had completed high school in Japan, but she had not learned English. Very few issei lived in Reno, which meant she couldn't talk to most people in town. Even dressing herself was a challenge. "I didn't know how to wear dresses and shoes properly," said Miyasaki. "Sometimes I wore my clothes oddly, and it was funny."[7]

Miyasaki thought hard about returning to Japan in 1918. But friends convinced her family to move to Sacramento, California. There they found a large Japanese community. Miyasaki learned English by taking classes at a local church.

▲ **Many Japanese immigrants started small businesses such as delis and restaurants.**

Some disappointed women sought divorce. But Noji, Endow, and Miyasaki stayed in the United States. Soon they had children to take care of. By being born in the United States, their children became U.S. citizens. They grew up surrounded by American culture. However, most of the issei themselves were not allowed to become citizens.

Chapter 4

TREATED LIKE THE ENEMY

December 7, 1941, was a sunny morning in Hawaii. Yasutaro Soga relaxed in his kimono on his front porch. It had been 45 years since he arrived on a steamship as a young man. World War II (1939–1945) had been going on for two years, but the United States was not involved. Soga read a magazine, as he often did on Sunday mornings.

Soga's telephone rang. The person on the other end told him that Japan had attacked nearby Pearl Harbor. Soga didn't believe it.

He turned on the radio. The announcer barked a stream of orders. "Keep calm," the announcer said. "The United States Army Intelligence has ordered that all civilians stay off the streets."[9] Japanese planes had surprised the U.S. fleet in Hawaii, destroying much of it. Soga wondered what that meant for himself and the many Japanese immigrants in Hawaii.

Later that day, in Hood River, Oregon, Itsu Akiyama watched a large number of American planes fly over her fruit trees. On the radio, people talked about the United States entering the war. Akiyama worried about her husband, who was head of the local Japanese society.

In the darkness of the next morning, headlights shone through their windows, waking Akiyama and her husband. Then they heard a knock on the door. When her husband opened it, they saw a government official and a police officer. These men yelled at Akiyama's husband and took him away to jail.

The United States declared war on Japan that day. Following that, the U.S. government arrested hundreds of Japanese leaders.

On February 19, 1942, President Franklin D. Roosevelt ordered 120,000 Japanese Americans to relocate to internment camps. Most were American citizens.

"It was awfully hot out there. To keep cool, I used to soak my feet in a bucket of water—and it was just awful standing in line at mealtime with dishes in our hands. When the wind was a little bit too much, a terrible dust storm came along with it. Dust was one of our biggest problems. However tight we shut the doors and windows, the dust came in the house and all over the inside."

—Hanayo Inouye, who was at an internment camp in Arizona during World War II[11]

On May 13, the time came for all Japanese Americans in Hood River to leave. Wearing numbered tags, Akiyama and her children carried their suitcases to the train station. The rest of their belongings had been sold or left in their home. "There were many Caucasian people to see us off," said Akiyama. "We had to wonder whether they were sincere in our leaving or maybe they were wishing we would never come back."[10]

The train moved slowly and reached its destination in the dark. Watchtowers loomed overhead.

▲ **Japanese Americans arrive at an internment camp in 1942.**

Searchlights showed barbed-wire fences and cacti. Armed guards stood on the other side of the fence. The Japanese families had arrived in a dry place. They waded through tall grass to reach flimsy houses.

The Japanese settled into camp life. Although the U.S. government provided necessities, many people still chose to work. Wages were low. Camp schools ran low on teachers and school supplies. Meanwhile, approximately 33,000 children of the issei joined the U.S. military.

Japanese Americans were set free after the United States and its **allies** won the war. Chiochi Nitta's family returned to their house in Loomis, California. A white family had been renting the house. Many dishes and all the farm tools were gone. Nitta's family had to move into the upstairs while they waited for the renters to leave.

The renters had stopped paying, and they were unhappy giving back the beds and refrigerator. In town, one of the stores displayed a sign that said no Japanese were allowed. As a result of losing property and facing **discrimination** in their old communities, many Japanese Americans moved to new states to start new lives.

Slowly, public opinion on issei began to change. In 1952, the United States reopened its doors to Japanese immigrants. At the same time, the issei were finally allowed to become U.S. citizens. In 1988, the U.S. government apologized for putting Japanese Americans in camps, and survivors received money.

For decades, the issei lived as strangers in their adopted country. Most of the issei embraced the chance to become citizens. Now they and their children, like so many immigrants before them, could become full members of the United States.

The Heart Mountain camp was turned into a museum in 2011. ▶

Chapter 5

PITCHING TO AMERICA

Shigetoshi Hasegawa couldn't take his eyes off the TV. Like many people in Japan, he was watching the Major League Baseball debut of Hideo Nomo. Nomo had been a star pitcher in Japan. But now, in 1995, he was playing in the United States.

Hasegawa understood why Nomo left. Hasegawa was a star pitcher for the Orix BlueWave in Kobe, Japan. He wanted the same thing Nomo did. He wanted to try his luck in the United States.

In 1997, Hasegawa got his chance. He signed with the Anaheim Angels. His dream had come true, but he felt very alone. He was working on his English, but he still didn't know enough to communicate with his teammates. "My first year, I was so alone. Nobody could talk to me," he said.[12]

Hasegawa passed the time in team hotels, unable to speak the most basic requests. Even baseball-related communication was tough. Hasegawa had been a starting pitcher in Japan. But he couldn't speak to the manager about wanting to remain a starter.

Hasegawa didn't have a translator, so he had to tackle the challenge on his own. He immersed himself in the language and worked hard. "You have to be brave," he said of learning English. "You have to have confidence."[13]

By 2002, Hasegawa's work had paid off. He was fluent in English. He had even written a book about teaching the language to Japanese people. As Hasegawa's language skills advanced, so did his professional baseball career. Hasegawa was playing for the Seattle Mariners, where he had two Japanese teammates. He was finally feeling comfortable with baseball—and with life in the United States.

▲ **Hasegawa finished his major league career with 447 strikeouts.**

Baseball was Hasegawa's passion, but he had a simpler reason for coming to the United States. "Hideo (Nomo), he had the dream of playing baseball right here, testing himself against the best," Hasegawa said. "And I wanted that challenge, too. But it was not really my dream. My dream was to live here."[14]

Hasegawa retired from baseball in 2005. In 2016, he joined the staff of his old Japanese team. But he worked from his home in the United States. He is a team adviser on foreign players.

When a reporter asked him to name his favorite thing about the United States, Hasegawa had an easy answer. "Everything," Hasegawa said. "That's why I live here."[15]

THINK ABOUT IT

- Why do you think many immigrants were willing to leave part of their family in Japan when they moved to the United States? What would you have done if you were in their situation?
- What are some things that surprised many issei about life in the United States? If you were in their position, how would you have handled it?
- What are some of the ways that life in the internment camps was difficult? How would you have felt if your family had been sent to one?
- Do you think most of the issei found what they were looking for in the United States? Why or why not?

GLOSSARY

allies (AL-ahyz): Allies are countries that fight on the same side in a war. The United States and its allies were victorious in World War II.

contract labor (KAHN-trakt LAY-bur): Contract labor is when workers are brought into a country to work for a specific employer. Many early Japanese immigrants worked as contract labor in Hawaii.

discrimination (dis-krim-i-NAY-shun): Discrimination is unfair behavior toward someone because of a difference such as race or gender. Japanese immigrants often experienced discrimination in the United States.

internment camps (in-TURN-ment KAMPS): Internment camps are places where large groups of people are confined without being found guilty of a crime. More than 100,000 Japanese Americans were forced to live in internment camps during World War II.

issei (EE-say): The issei are Japanese immigrants. The issei started many Japanese communities on the West Coast.

manure (muh-NOOR): Manure is animal waste that is used as fertilizer. White teenagers threw manure at Mitsumori.

migratory (MY-gruh-tor-ee): Migratory means moving from one place to another. Migratory workers moved from farm to farm hoping to find work.

plantations (plan-TAY-shuhnz): Plantations are large farms where valuable crops are tended by people living on-site. Many immigrants to Hawaii started by working on sugar plantations.

quarantine (KWOR-uhn-teen): A quarantine is a way of keeping people, animals, or plants apart from others to control the spread of disease. Immigrants had to go through a quarantine process before they could start their new lives.

SOURCE NOTES

1. Yukiko Kimura. *Issei: Japanese Immigrants in Hawaii*. Honolulu, HI: University of Hawaii Press, 1988. Print. 12.

2. Ronald T. Takaki. *Strangers from a Different Shore: A History of Asian Americans*. Boston, MA: Little, Brown, 1998. Print. 74.

3. Eileen Sunada Sarasohn, ed. *The Issei, Portrait of a Pioneer: An Oral History*. Palo Alto, CA: Pacific Books, 1983. Print. 59.

4. Ibid. 76.

5. Linda Tamura. *The Hood River Issei: An Oral History of Japanese Settlers in Oregon's Hood River Valley*. Chicago, IL: University of Illinois Press, 1993. Print. 36.

6. Ibid. 56.

7. Eileen Sunada Sarasohn, ed. *The Issei, Portrait of a Pioneer: An Oral History*. Palo Alto, CA: Pacific Books, 1983. Print. 125.

8. Ibid. 112.

9. Yukiko Kimura. *Issei: Japanese Immigrants in Hawaii*. Honolulu, HI: University of Hawaii Press, 1988. Print. 215.

10. Linda Tamura. *The Hood River Issei: An Oral History of Japanese Settlers in Oregon's Hood River Valley*. Chicago, IL: University of Illinois Press, 1993. Print. 167.

11. Eileen Sunada Sarasohn, ed. *The Issei, Portrait of a Pioneer: An Oral History*. Palo Alto, CA: Pacific Books, 1983. Print. 196.

12. Jim Caple. "More Than an Ocean Divide." *ESPN*. ESPN Internet Ventures, 12 May 2002. Web. 25 Jan. 2017.

13. Ibid.

14. Dave Wielenga. "Gettin Shig-ee with It." *OC Weekly*. OC Weekly, 14 Sept. 2000. Web. 25 Jan. 2017.

15. "Take Five with . . . Shigetoshi Hasegawa." *Seattle Post-Intelligencer*. Hearst Seattle Media, 30 Mar. 2004. Web. 25 Jan. 2017.

TO LEARN MORE

Books

Demuth, Patricia Brennan. *What Was Pearl Harbor?* New York, NY: Grosset & Dunlap, 2013.

Freedman, Russell. *Angel Island: Gateway to Gold Mountain*. New York, NY: Clarion Books, 2014.

Marrin, Albert. *Uprooted: The Japanese American Experience during World War II*. New York, NY: Alfred A. Knopf, 2016.

Web Sites

Visit our Web site for links about Japanese immigrants:
childsworld.com/links

Note to Parents, Teachers, and Librarians: We routinely verify our Web links to make sure they are safe and active sites. So encourage your readers to check them out!

INDEX